Development and Management of Research Groups

Development
and Management
of Research Groups

A Guide for University Researchers

by Robert V. Smith

Illustrations by Sally Blakemore

University of Texas Press   Austin and London

Library of Congress Cataloging in Publication Data

Smith, Robert V   1942–
    Development and management of research groups.

    Bibliography: p.
    1. Research—United States—Management.   I. Title.
Q180.U5S393   001.4'3   79-23097
ISBN 0-292-71523-4
ISBN 0-292-71524-2 pbk.

Requests for permission to reproduce material from this work should be
sent to Permissions, University of Texas Press, Box 7819, Austin, Texas
78712.

To my loving and understanding wife, Denene

Contents

Preface

This book is written for professorial research managers of small research groups. I define "small" as a group consisting of ten or fewer full-time-equivalent (FTE) research personnel. While the principles and guidelines suggested may apply also to larger research teams, my experience has generally been confined to "small" groups. Besides university researchers, this book may also be of benefit to graduate and postdoctoral students intending to pursue academic careers.

During the past five years, I have been associated administratively with a drug research institute housed in a college of pharmacy at a major state university. This association has provided numerous opportunities to investigate techniques for motivating researchers and managing scientific studies, which included grant and contract research funded by foundations, governmental bodies, and private industry. Research in our institute involves biological and chemical investigations; thus, our experiences are most applicable to researchers in the natural sciences.

Both subtle and profound changes have occurred in the research establishment of the United States during the 1970's. Increasing fiscal restraints and inflation have decreased real-dollar support to research endeavors over the past ten years. At the same time, the number of researchers seeking funding has escalated, primarily due to increases in faculty size during the student-growth period of the 1960's. This increase has forced grant-review and funding groups to be more priority conscious. Simultaneously, professional research administrators in government and industry have become more committed to the principles of management by objectives. The professorial researcher today must maximize productivity to be consistently effective in attracting outside funding.

In recent years, emphasis has been placed on multidisciplinary and interdisciplinary research efforts, thus presenting a twofold challenge to the professorial researcher. First, research teams must be developed that include individuals outside any single area of expertise. Second, management techniques are required that will promote greater and greater effectiveness. Furthermore, reporting mechanisms for researchers have become more complex. Unfortunately, academicians tend to be suspicious of management techniques, which may be perceived as stifling or counter to the freedom that may have been sought in a university-based career. However, it is my view that good management practices are currently necessary for the survival of any research effort. The alternative is to be buried in paper work, unable to meet research objectives.

The university researcher can be eclectic in his/her selection of management techniques, which has been my approach in preparing this book.

Some suggestions and guidelines contained herein may seem so basic that the reader might think that these are matters of "common sense." I accept that possible liability for the sake of assisting the novice research manager. At the same time, I have attempted to make this volume sufficiently brief so that a greater number of researchers may spend a few valuable hours assimilating its message and effecting those recommendations that seem most useful to their research teams. It is my hope that this book may aid the research manager in the always more challenging task of developing and managing university-based research groups.

My research program has been aided by a number of grants and contracts over the past five years. These awards have indirectly supported the preparation of this volume and I gratefully acknowledge the National Institute of Neurological and Communicative Disorders and Stroke, National Institutes of Health (grant NS-12259), the U.S. Food and Drug Administration (contract 223-75-3004), the Robert A. Welch Foundation (grant F-690), the World Health Organization (research training grant MS/181/4B.158), and Hoffman LaRoche, Inc., for their support. I am also indebted to Dr. Alfred Martin, founding director of the Drug Dynamics Institute, and to Dr. James T. Doluisio, Dean of the College of Pharmacy, University of Texas at Austin, for their encouragement and help. I am also thankful to the American Management Association for instructional materials that were made available to me through a course offered by the Personnel Department at the University of Texas at Austin. Marilyn Buchanan is acknowledged for the excellent stenographic work she contributed to this manuscript. I am also grateful to Michael Dews for his superb copy-editing skills. Finally, and by no means of least importance, I acknowledge the many faculty, students, and postdoctoral associates who have contributed to research programs in the Drug Dynamics Institute over the past half-decade.

Robert V. Smith

Developing the
Research Group

1

Obtaining Grant Support

Few departments or universities have sufficient resources to finance high-quality research programs. Excellence must be bought extramurally by the research manager.* Funds are needed for researchers'** salaries and wages, as well as for expendable supplies, chemicals, equipment, office supplies, computer time, animals and their maintenance, and, in some cases, wages for office staff. Faculty and others commonly refer to "grants" as sources of research funds; however, there are a number of recognized vehicles for supporting university research activities. These are listed below:
1. Free gift
2. Grant
3. Contract
4. Fellowship
5. Scholarship

*Hereafter used as a designation for the professorial researcher in charge of two or more researchers.

**All undergraduate, graduate, and postdoctoral students and technicians reporting to the research manager.

A free gift implies no accountability. Nevertheless, bene-
factors usually have a purpose for contributing to a research
program and the research manager should be able to describe (though not necessarily in strictest terms) the expenditure of these funds. Universities often designate a free gift as
any sum of money for which no specific objective need to be
met and no formal reports to the donor need to be made.
Free gifts may be acquired through alumni foundation efforts
or may sometimes be requested from long-time industrial
contractors who may have been particularly pleased with
efforts of the research manager and his/her group during
previous contractual arrangements (see below).

One has the greatest degree of flexibility when spending
free gift money. However, it is the hardest money to raise and
will rarely provide the substantive support needed to develop a significant program.

A grant is described as a flexible instrument which a
sponsor uses to stimulate or fund research activity or to
encourage other, worthwhile endeavors, such as the purchase of equipment, construction of facilities, or convening a
professional meeting. Ideas for a grant request generally
come from the research manager or from members of
her/his group. The scope of the project is also defined by the
research manager. A grant usually allows some freedom to
alter objectives. However, grants require accountability, both
in the expenditure of funds and in the conduct of research.
In fact, granting agencies have become more aware, in
recent years, of the need for stated objectives and now
demand evidence of attempts to meet these objectives during
the course of the award. This is especially true for federally
sponsored grants and it places heavy responsibility on the
shoulders of the research manager.

Mission-oriented, or focused, grant projects tend to inhibit more open-ended basic research efforts. The lack of a sense of accountability, however, which university researchers may have experienced in the past, is no longer compatible with continued success in securing outside grant support, particularly from the federal government.

A research contract is an agreement to perform specific work which is defined relatively carefully. Thus, there is not as much flexibility for the research manager working with contractual support as there is for one who sustains his/her research through grants. Federal contracts are issued following the appearance of a Request for Proposal (RFP) notice in the *Commerce Business Daily*. The research manager may write to the relevant federal agency to receive an RFP. The nomenclature in many procedures required by the federal government is confusing, and the RFP process is no exception. The "actual" RFP (formally sent to the research manager) is a document which outlines the objectives of the contract, criteria for selecting the contractor, and some guidelines for constructing a budget. The latter are given in terms of the government's estimate of the number of man-years (equivalent to the number of men/women working full time for one year) required to fulfill the objectives of the contract. Occasionally, RFP's have such specific objectives that they seem to have been written by an investigator already working in the area, which may be a clue that the contract is already activated. Contracts, like grants, come up periodically for competitive renewal. At such times they will be described in the *Commerce Business Daily* and can be bid upon by any number of qualified investigators. The research manager has no way, except through intuition, to know whether the RFP is of the type described. In cases of renewal contracts, the likelihood of the novice attaining funds can be, indeed, quite slim.

Industrial contracts, like their government counterparts, usually involve highly focused research and relatively little freedom to deviate from stated objectives. Industrial firms, however, may be a little more generous in this respect than federal agencies.

Government agencies are required by law to award contracts to the lowest bidder and often engage in vigorous negotiation over the amount of money awarded to the institution. Sometimes, research managers may be tempted to underbid in time of financial need even though research programs will utimately suffer as a result. Furthermore, a gross underestimation of the funds necessary to complete a project will damage the credibility of the research manager in the eyes of reviewers.

Occasionally, a research manager's application for a research grant will stimulate the initiation of an RFP. This may lead to a combination grant/contract award to the research manager, which is preferable to a contract alone. If there is a choice between the contract or grant, I prefer the grant because of its flexibility.

Fellowships are awards which support the advanced or continued education of scholars or researchers. Generally, fellowships are offered to predoctoral or postdoctoral students. The majority of government-sponsored programs go to the postdoctoral people. Especially bright postdoctoral students should be encouraged to apply for fellowships, such as those available from the National Institutes of Health and the National Science Foundation. Information on these programs is available at sponsored projects offices on campus or from the agencies themselves (see Chapter 8 for more on this subject).

Scholarships are generally awarded to undergraduates and so will have small impact on the research manager's program. A notable exception is an award from the Undergraduate Research Participation (URP) program sponsored by the National Science Foundation. Grants made through this program provide summer support for undergraduate students between their second and third or third and fourth years in college. In addition to stipend support, the URP awards include laboratory supply expenses, and they can be structured to support modest travel requests. The URP grants are of great benefit in introducing research to undergraduates who may be interested in pursuing graduate study. Awards generally involve more than one supervisory professor, and the research manager will have to collaborate with colleagues in related disciplines to prepare appropriate proposals.

Many universities have seed-grant programs which may allocate up to $5,000 during a calendar year to help professorial researchers launch new projects. These grants provide an excellent way of collecting enough data to prepare more formidable grant proposals to be sent to governmental agencies or to industry. While there is no substitute for a good idea or thesis in developing a proposal, a working hypothesis is significantly strengthened if preliminary supporting data can be obtained. The seed-grant mechanism often permits this.

The research manager should send her/his grant proposals to any agency which might conceivably be interested in supporting the project. Of course, neither private nor public agencies will be happy about duplicating support. Thus, it behooves the research manager to be completely honest and to clearly state in competing proposals that funding for one will automatically cause self-initiated withdrawal of the other.

A number of books and articles are available which

describe the specific application requirements and review processes for federal grants (see Bibliography), and exact details need not be duplicated here. Additional information is available from agencies and institutes, and the prospective grantee is encouraged to make telephone contacts to determine interest in specific projects. Pertinent telephone numbers are listed in the Federal Directory, which is available through any university library. Some recommendations can be made regarding strategies. There is a blend of realism and persistence necessary during the pursuit of grant funding before the research manager enters the ranks of successful grant recipients. A grant is frequently not funded on its first "go-around." It may have to be modified in some way to make it more competitive. There are also times when it is best to give up on a proposal. This is probably most true in cases of outright rejection or when the proposal has been approved but given a very low priority more than once.

Fortunately, the federal grant-review process has become more open in recent years. Peer-review summaries are available to research managers, along with priority scores. Thus, good feedback is available from which to decide whether or not to continue to seek funds for a project. A turndown from an industrial firm is usually final, and reapplication is likely to be an exercise in futility.

In later sections (Chapters 6 and 8), difficulties which novice researchers have in beginning their careers are described, as are the anxiety and frustrations these individuals face after initial efforts in the laboratory. The new professorial researcher or research manager faces similar difficulties in securing funds for his/her programs and only hard work, persistence, and a constant striving for high scholarly goals will lead to success.

During experiments which preceed actual grant pro-

posals, the research manager may want to enlist co-investigators, who are frequently professorial colleagues from one's own or related departments. Alignments of this nature should come about naturally and should be sensible in terms of the project's objectives. Occasionally, administrative superiors try to encourage internal collaborative efforts with a particular professor who may not have been active for some time or whose strengths have not been documented. These collaborative efforts may be futile and can place the joint grant proposal in jeopardy. It is good to keep in mind that reviewers see through weak, phony, or politically motivated collaborative efforts, and false alignments of this sort should be assiduously avoided.

On the positive side, a co-investigator who is bright and enthusiastic and has a clearly relevant (even though modest in quantity) record of accomplishments will prove to be an asset to a grant proposal. The research manager who pursues multidisciplinary or interdisciplinary research will, no doubt, want to collaborate with individuals whose strengths are complementary to her/his own.

Because the terms "multidisciplinary" and "interdisciplinary" research are used throughout this book, they need to be defined.

Interdisciplinary research involves the joint, coordinated, and continuously integrated efforts of investigators from different disciplinary backgrounds. These people work together to produce results which are so tightly woven that individual contributions are not easily identified. In chemical-biological interdisciplinary studies, for example, the chemist will perform biological experiments; the biologist will do some chemical work.

Multidisciplinary research results from experts in different disciplines working separately on various aspects of a primary objective. The synthesis of results is done primarily by the research manager.

Interdisciplinary efforts are more difficult to manage than multidisciplinary work; however, the rewards can be greater. The terms "multidisciplinary" and "interdisciplinary" are frequently used loosely. Many so-called interdisciplinary investigations are, in fact, hybrids.

The research manager who prepares proposals which encourage interdisciplinary or multidisciplinary efforts must carefully explain how she/he will manage such work. For example, in research grant applications submitted to the National Institutes of Health there is a section on collaborative arrangements in which the applicant is requested to describe how he/she will coordinate the efforts of several investigators and outside collaborators. A description of some recommendations made in the subsequent management section of this book could be employed in preparing such a section (see, especially, Chapters 4, 7, and 8).

Many peer reviewers of federal grants and contracts tend to be suspicious of interdisciplinary or multidisciplinary research, based on their own backgrounds. Peer reviewers typically will also be biased by the framework of universities and colleges. Academic institutions primarily have a disciplinary basis for their structure; for example, there are departments of chemistry, biology, English, history and so on. This structure, along with guidelines which are established and followed by professors seeking tenure and promotion, tends to emphasize individual and discipline-based work.

A research institute or interdisciplinary team of workers is mission oriented. Flexibility and imagination are key elements which motivate these groups. The peer reviewer who has practiced a different "brand" of research over the years will have to be convinced that the interdisciplinary approach is fitting to the particular problem addressed. Collaborative arrangements must be very carefully developed.

Up to this point, attention has been focused on federal grants and contracts. This was done because the guidelines and problems associated with these agencies are relatively clear. If one errs, either in approach or in the assumption that a certain study is worthy of funding, there is feedback. This is not necessarily true with proposals submitted to foundations and industrial firms. These bodies have no responsibility to the applicant and need not justify a rejected proposal. Particularly when dealing with foundations, one will face idiosyncratic and often restrictive application and administration procedures. The research manager must thus exercise special care when dealing with foundations.

While there are no set procedures for applying to foundations, it is generally advisable to contact these agencies in

writing prior to submittal of a formal proposal. The initial contact letter briefly answers the following questions, as recently outlined by V. P. White (see Bibliography):

1. What is to be done?
2. Why is it worth doing?
3. What are the specific objectives?
4. Who is to do the work?
5. What facilities will be required and are they available?
6. How long will the project take?
7. About how much will the project cost?
8. Can a full proposal be submitted?

The research manager should send a curriculum vitae or a short biographical sketch along with the initial contact letter to the foundation. A full proposal should only be forwarded when interest is expressed. A negative letter or no response from a foundation makes further effort unnecessary. There are about five thousand foundations in the United States with assets of $500,000 or more. These agencies annually award a number of grants over $5,000. Their locations and further hints on dealing with these groups are discussed in the references cited in the Bibliography. Approaches to industrial firms should follow a course similar to that outlined for research foundations. An important addition, however, must be added to the inquiry letter. The industrial firm will want to know how the research manager's proposal can be translated into profits.

It is wise to have some personal contact with key individuals in foundations and industrial firms. Establishing this is left to the ingenuity of the reader.

This volume is not intended to be a guidebook for preparing grants and contracts; however, some general thoughts on the subject are in order. A grant may be structured in many ways, but it is convenient to adopt and stay with one format, if possible. This facilitates sending grants to several agencies and making proposal revisions. I use the format of the National Institutes of Health research-grant application (NIH 398), which includes the following sections:

1. Cover page
2. Summary (with key words underlined)
3. Budget
4. Biographical sketches of investigators
5. Research plan
   A) Specific aims
   B) Significance and background
   C) Progress report or preliminary studies
   D) Methods
   E) Collaborative assurance
   F) Facilities available

This format is generally employed for foundation and industrial proposals; however, one should always adhere to format requirements (if these are available) for foundations. Additionally, foundations may be particularly pleased to see a layperson's summary (see also Chapter 15) of the proposed work for use in public relations activities. Proposals submitted to industry need only be logically developed in terms of format, and the one recommended above should suffice in most cases.

The impact of the narrative section of a grant is dependent upon the value of the research manager's ideas, as well as her/his ability to state those ideas in objective terms. The research manager must also achieve clarity of expression and thoroughness in discussions. Formulating the narrative section will, therefore, take many hours of careful preparation. The research manager may not need to give nearly as much thought to the preliminary sections of the proposal even though they may be of equal or even greater significance! Some reviewers will peruse the entire proposal; because of time constraints, many may only be able to read the summary and other preliminary pages. Thus, the summary or abstract should be highly effective. It must describe as succinctly as possible the objectives, methods, and significance of the proposal. It should be written only after the narrative is complete and the overall perspective of the proposal formulated.

The budget should be a realistic appraisal of the costs that the research manager anticipates in performing the study. It should include a minimum number of requests for major equipment, and those should be carefully justified. Most agencies are reluctant to support capital expenditures in research studies.

Salary allocation for the research manager should be in accord with the anticipated time commitment. Few, if any, major studies can be carried out without postdoctoral researchers, and one or more lines for these individuals should be incorporated into the budget. As the research manager develops a "track record" in managing research and formulating budgets, he/she gains a feeling for the amount of money it takes per FTE per year to do research. This estimate can be used in formulating expense allowances for expendable supplies and chemicals. In my experience, it is currently difficult to support a postdoctoral fellow or advanced graduate student on less than $5,000 per year for routine supplies, chemicals, and other laboratory expendables. This will, of course, vary with the type of project and is merely quoted as a benchmark.

If a subcontract is to be budgeted, its breakdown is given on a separate page. The total for the subcontracted work is included in the primary budget. Collaborative efforts with individuals at institutions outside the research manager's university system, where separate budgets are requested, will require approval of the composite proposal by respective institutions. There may be ways of expediting review if one belongs to a university system and collaboration is proposed by investigators at component institutions. Research managers should check on precise requirements at their sponsored projects office.

Biographical sketches should be included for all doctoral-level people who will contribute to the proposed project. These should be no longer than two or three pages and should include a list of all publications (with titles) which are relevant to the proposed project. The biographical materials should clearly indicate the relationship of each person to the project.

Appendices may be added to grant proposals. These may include preprints of manuscripts, reports, charts or photos of facilities (if the latter play a particularly important role in the proposal, such as studies including manufacturing activities), and letters of intent. If collaborators (see Chapter 4) are willing to serve as gratis consultants to a project, their contributions should be documented by letters appended to the proposal.

2

Recruiting Personnel

The aphorism about the group being only as good as the individuals in it is quite applicable to research. Attracting funds and recruiting outstanding researchers are two very important functions of a good research manager. As will be noted in later chapters (especially Chapter 8), postdoctoral researchers can make the greatest contribution to one's research effort. Also, the most logistical effort must be expended to recruit these individuals because they must be exclusively enlisted by the research manager and they will usually come from other universities.

Technicians are often recruited through university personnel offices. University towns frequently attract recent graduates who want to settle where they studied, and an abundance of baccalaureate students who are willing to work at salary levels commensurate with technical help are often available. One disadvantage of these people is that they may not be working at capacity and will likely remain in the group for only a year or two. The research manager will often face high turnover rates with technical help.

The pool from which to choose graduate students to join

the research team is affected by the recruiting efforts of the research manager's parent department or college. Research managers with funding for research assistantships can do some independent recruiting through colleagues around the country. Students who join a college or department may frequently spend an academic term taking courses and trying to decide which professor (research manager) to choose as principal advisor. Indeed, departments should encourage new graduate students to visit with all professorial members so that they can make a more informed choice of major professor. The well-funded professorial research manager who provides leadership in his/her group as outlined in the second part of this book will have a good chance of attracting the better candidates.

Postdoctoral students are recruited in several ways. The research manager may receive an unsolicited letter from a graduate student who anticipates finishing her/his Ph.D. soon and who has, through literature readings or discussions with an advisor, been intrigued by the research manager's activities. If this inquiry comes when a position will soon be available, one is in luck. More often than not, it will not be that easy to recruit postdoctoral students. I have made contacts over an eleven-year period with professorial colleagues in perhaps two dozen major universities around the country. When a postdoctoral position is open, a personal letter is sent to each of these individuals. The letter very briefly describes the position and quotes an approximate salary level. It expresses interest in recruiting an individual from the contacted colleague's research group or from those of other faculty persons in the colleague's department. Any student the colleague thinks might be interested is instructed to apply in writing and to supply a curriculum vitae and the names of three individuals who are familiar with the student's research capabilities. This approach, more often than not, attracts suitable candidates. When it does not, the research manager should advertise for postdoctoral students in trade magazines or journals. *Chemical and Engineering News*, published by the American Chemical Society, and *Science*, published by the American Association for the Advancement of Science, are widely read and will attract inquiries from people in the chemical and biological sciences.

Once a promising individual has applied for the postdoctoral position in the group, an acknowledgment letter may be returned with a statement to the effect that the research manager is proceeding with their application. Applications from individuals with apparently weaker backgrounds should be held temporarily. Rather than ask for formal letters of recommendation, I have found it more useful and expeditious to telephone for references. During the telephone interview, questions should be raised about the strengths of the candidate. As a guide, I use a "question sheet" like the one reproduced here.

Question Sheet Used to Obtain Telephone
Recommendations for Candidates for Postdoctoral Positions

Question Type   *Notes*
   1. Laboratory technique;
      organization; special skills?
   2. Creativeness; contributes ideas
      to projects; love of science?
   3. Writing and speaking abilities?
   4. Familiarity with the literature?
   5. Career objective?
   6. Bright; intelligent; catches on quickly?
   7. Punctual in assignments?

8. Takes orders cheerfully?
9. Reliability?
10. Pleasantness?
11. Trustworthiness?
12. Can work under pressure?
13. Easy to work with?
14. Works well with others?
15. Sickness record?
16. Brings problems from home?
17. What are shortcomings?

Sometimes, references are overly kind in their assessment of the candidate and may volunteer no negative feelings. In such instances, I may say, "All of us have faults. If you had to give just one shortcoming of candidate X, what would it be?" This can "break the ice" and help the research manager obtain a more balanced evaluation of a candidate.

Once the research manager has located the right person for the job, that person should be contacted by telephone to determine her/his continued interest in the position. Candidates living within a certain radius can be invited for an interview. If he/she lives at a great distance and travel funds are limited, the research manager will need to decide about making an offer based on the information gathered.

An offer made over the telephone should be quickly followed by a written proposal. Since the postdoctoral candidate may be considering a number of offers, the research manager's letter should present the offer as positively as possible. I usually describe the position in some detail. A salary quotation is made along with a short description of fringe benefits. Some information on the university is offered and a description is made of the local environs. At the end of the letter, a request can be made that notice of acceptance

be communicated within a period of ten days. If the offer is rejected, there is still time to contact other applicants.

I keep a file which contains a number of items useful in recruiting postdoctoral students. Articles emphasizing the attractions and advantages of the locale can be influential in attracting recruits to the group. Data sheets containing such information as city size, weather, cost of living, and other vital statistics are helpful.

Once the postdoctoral recruit has accepted the offer, be ready to facilitate the move he/she might have to make. While few grants provide support for moving expenses, the research manager can meet other needs. A letter to the Chamber of Commerce can gain local information for the new recruit. Usually, I invite new postdoctoral students to spend the first couple of days in my home until an apartment or other permanent residence can be secured. New personnel show great appreciation for this type of hospitality. During this visit, the research manager and postdoctoral student can become better acquainted and the student can be advised concerning the in's and out's of the local housing market.

3

Procuring Equipment and Instrumentation Services

Experiments in the natural sciences, particularly in biology, chemistry, and physics, require a wide variety of electronic equipment. In spite of this, funds for permanent equipment are usually the most difficult to raise. Permanent equipment is typically defined as an apparatus costing more than $1,000. In some federal grants, research managers have the option of purchasing less costly items from the "other expenses" category of their budgets. More expensive equipment may require the approval of a university central administrative officer or a granting agency official. Approval for budget changes leading to equipment purchases must be obtained when work is sponsored by federal contract. The research manager should always check with his/her sponsored projects office before changing the budget to purchase equipment.

The National Science Foundation (NSF) sponsors a number of programs in which application can be made to purchase major items of equipment. These programs are described in an NSF brochure listed in the reference section of this book. One NSF program (Institutional Equipment

Program) is concerned with educational objectives in undergraduate courses or programs. It is an excellent way to obtain
apparatus which can serve the research, as well as the
teaching, missions of the research manager. In fact, the
research manager should generally try to combine research
and teaching objectives in this way. If a laboratory course is
part of one's responsibility, two goals can be served if equipment for teaching can also benefit research.

While attending national professional meetings, research managers should investigate instrumentation exhibits.
Manufacturer's representatives at these gatherings are eager
to demonstrate their company's equipment and to subsequently forward descriptive literature. The research manager
should insist on receiving accompanying price information
even though the latter may quickly go out of date. Laboratory
guides to equipment and vendors are published yearly by the
American Chemical Society and the American Association
for the Advancement of Science through their journals, *Ana-
lytical Chemistry* and *Science*, respectively. These publications are also sources of instrumentation manufacturers'
phone numbers, which can be used to quickly obtain information or price quotations.

Research managers with research grants from the NSF
may request equipment through surplus equipment pools,
which are managed by the agency and which involve costs
limited to shipment of items from current storage points. The
eligible research manager should work with his/her university procurement officer in obtaining equipment from this
source.

Occasionally, there are opportunities for departments or
institutes to combine resources in order to purchase major
pieces of equipment. Arrangements may also be made to
create full-time staff lines to pay for individuals who operate

particularly delicate and difficult-to-maintain apparatus. Such transactions often represent the most efficient use of funds. Nevertheless, there should be clear understanding before resources are committed. Agreements will include times which are allotted to each partner, commitments for continuing operator salary support, the purchase of routine supplies, and guidelines for establishing service fees.

Developing the Research Group

The research manager should maintain a file of equipment descriptions which she/he would like to purchase in the future. Occasionally, departments have "surplus funds" at the end of a fiscal year which may require quick expenditure. The research manager with a request that can be processed rapidly often has an advantage over those who might have to formulate a request. One way to promote current awareness of new apparatus is to arrange periodic instrument demonstrations by local sales persons in the laboratory which have been coordinated by the instrument specialist (see Chapter 12).

Some universities purchase equipment with a percentage of overhead funds from grants or from other, unspecified federal moneys (e.g., additional funds available to departments which attract grants greater than $200,000 per year from the National Institutes of Health). The research manager should determine how these moneys are distributed. If a faculty committee is involved, the research manager should seek out the committee chairperson and question him/her on the proper means of making requests.

4

Developing Collaborative Arrangements

In-house collaborators or co-investigators have already been discussed. The research manager should encourage input from co-investigators during grant preparations and following the implementation of funded awards. Indeed, the input of co-investigators will strengthen their commitment.

Collaborations with investigators outside the research manager's university are not as easily arranged as with colleagues on campus. The research manager's reputation may take years to develop to the extent that it elicits requests from colleagues at other institutes to seek collaboration. Similarly, contacts initiated by the research manager with other researchers about possible collaborative work will probably meet with success when she/he has established a record of excellence.

Collaboration with off-campus experts can greatly strengthen research projects, particularly if the collaborating individuals have strong credentials and are widely respected. During collaboration there must be a willingness to share data prior to publication. Additionally, close communication will be necessary to avoid redundancy in experimentation.

Developing the Research Group

Work resulting from collaborative efforts may be published jointly. The research manager should realize that this may be a lengthy process and that certain compromises in the methods used to express results or approaches will often be required. In all joint publication efforts (see also Chapter 10) there should be one author who is primarily responsible for handling the final draft as well as corresponding with editors. Before a project begins, agreement should be reached on first-author status and relative responsibilities of contribution. An additional "rule of thumb" is that only those who actively contribute to a study be recognized as authors of resultant papers.

The research manager who prepares a grant proposal which includes collaborative work should carefully describe these arrangements in his/her proposal (see Chapter 1). Granting agencies usually request the verification of each collaborator's contribution. These typically consist of letters included in the appendices and obtained from collaborators.

Managing the
Research Group

5

Orientation of Personnel

Research personnel, regardless of whether they are graduate students, technicians, or postdoctoral students, deserve an honest explanation of what is expected of them during their tenure in the group. Orientation sessions can serve this purpose. At these meetings information can also be provided on fringe benefits and staff privileges.

Many universities conduct orientation meetings for new employees through their personnel departments. The research manager, however, should be prepared to answer inquiries about university-provided fringe benefits. He/she should also review requirements and privileges unique to the department or research institute.

Student researchers have special needs for information. For example, graduate and postdoctoral students may have to contribute to a retirement program during their tenure in the research group. It is good for them to know if these funds are recoverable upon termination of employment. A postdoctoral student who serves one to three years in the group and contributes 6–10 percent of his/her salary to a retirement plan will accumulate sufficient funds to cover moving

expenses that may be incurred when he/she moves on to a permanent position. If the student is inclined to tap such funds (and most will, in my experience), they provide excellent "insurance."

During the first orientation session the new researcher is informed of available secretarial services. The new employee should also be introduced to all staff members with whom

he/she will be in frequent contact. This is particularly important in the case of purchasing-department staff since procurement responsibilities will soon be delegated to the new
researcher (see Chapter 11). The novice researcher should
also be helped to secure parking privileges. Individualized
memoranda to appropriate university-staff personnel from
the research manager are helpful in obtaining the most
efficient and courteous service. At the initial orientation
meeting, the research manager may wish to review good
laboratory notebook procedures with the new researcher
(see Chapter 8). Finally, the researcher should be escorted to
his/her laboratory, and specific space assignments should be
made. I consider it appropriate for each researcher to have a
desk in close proximity to the laboratory bench. The researcher should also have his/her own bookshelf and at least
one filing cabinet. Office supplies should be available in
each laboratory.

University personnel departments may produce newslet-
ters for staff employees which will periodically contain information helpful to researchers in the group. The research
manager may wish to maintain a file with general personnel
information of this type which can be selectively photo-
copied and used during orientation sessions. The general
personnel folder should also be used to retain information on
changes in policy for hiring or terminating employees.

When a new technician or student researcher is hired or
joins the group, it is useful to prepare two file folders. Each is
marked with the individual's name; one is designated "personal," while the second is reserved for research reports (see
Chapter 6). The former file will be useful in saving copies of
memoranda to the employee, copies of appointment papers,
and letters of recommendations that will eventually be required when the researcher completes his/her studies. The

research report file provides ready access to information during manuscript and progress-report preparations.

During the first orientation meeting, the research manager should outline the research problems which will be assigned to the new employee (see Chapter 8). This is also a good time to provide the new researcher with copies of relevant publication reprints, recent progress reports, and perhaps a copy of a recent grant renewal application. The researcher is encouraged to read these documents and to return within the next two to three days with questions. At this subsequent meeting, more careful and detailed plans for the new researcher's initial experiments are discussed. During this second orientation session, the research manager's reporting requirements are outlined. I require all researchers, except undergraduates, to prepare a monthly research report in the style of a journal article (see Chapter 6). Attendance requirements at individual research and group meetings can also be described during this second orientation meeting (see also Chapter 6).

6

Reporting Mechanisms

There should be a balance of spontaneity and consistency in the relationship between the research manager and his/her student researchers and technicians. Researchers should participate in conferences planned by the research manager throughout the year. The research manager should also provide opportunities for daily contact with researchers (see Chapter 7).

A semester or quarter is a common time measurement in universities. Either of these provides the research manager three or four occasions every year in which to plan individual and group research conferences. Changes in arrangements or schedules are conveniently made between sessions. At the start of each quarter or semester, researchers are individually contacted by their research manager and their course schedules or other commitments for the forthcoming period are obtained. Once compiled, these schedules are used by the research manager to plan conferences for the entire quarter or semester. The needs of the researchers will vary; however, weekly or bi-weekly individual conferences are recommended. I try to schedule these conferences early in the morning and with no more than one conference per day. Thus, for a group of five to ten researchers, the research manager will be occupied nearly every day with one individual conference. This provides a reassuring sense of continuity for the research manager.

The individual research conferences serve an obvious communication need. They also exert subtle pressure on the researcher to accomplish certain objectives during the one-to-two-week intervals between conferences. This is, perhaps, not of great importance with postdoctoral researchers who are devoting full time to research. Graduate and undergraduate students, however, may be faced with significant course demands and will likely tend to put aside research during examination periods and while preparing term papers. While the research manager can empathize with these demands, some level of research activity should *always* be pursued. A lack of continuity in a student's research program can do significant harm, not only to his/her own training as a researcher, but also to the effort of the research group as a whole (see also Chapter 7).

Another advantage to planned individual research conferences is the support they offer to the relationship between research manager and researcher. The active research manager may spend a couple of months in a given year occupied with travel commitments. In spite of these necessary excursions by the research manager, the researcher is guaranteed a fixed number of conferences with his/her research manager every academic session. These meetings provide tangible evidence of the concern that the research manager has for the researcher and his/her accomplishments.

In interdisciplinary research efforts, occasional special joint conferences among two or three researchers of the group are advised. These sessions can be planned on an ad

hoc basis and are especially useful after initial efforts with unfamiliar techniques or experimental routines.

Of great importance to the research manager are monthly reports which are prepared by all levels of researchers, except perhaps undergraduates (see Chapter 8). These should be written in the style of a journal article with appropriate sections (i.e., cover page with researcher's name, affiliation, and date; introduction; experimental sections; results and discussions; and references) and should be due at a designated time each month. I prefer the first day of the month. This monthly report emphasizes the need for accountability in one's research group. Furthermore, it serves as a model for an activity which all researchers will face in the "real world."

The research manager must stress care and completeness in the preparation of the monthly report, especially in the experimental sections. A suggestion which I make to researchers is that suitably prepared experimental sections can often be lifted verbatim from a monthly report for use in the preparation of a manuscript or a dissertation. A conscientiously prepared monthly report serves a second purpose: its preparation forces the researcher to reflect upon the month's activities and to seriously confront difficult interpretations or apparent data anomalies. This thoughtful process frequently helps in planning new experiments, especially ones which may prove more definitive.

The monthly report may also contain appendices. For example, I encourage the researchers to prepare detailed instructions for routine determinations which may have recently been initiated in the laboratory. A newly adopted protein determination, for example, might be written up in a laboratory-manual style for subsequent use by technicians or other researchers in the group.

The research manager should correct the researcher's report soon after receiving it. At this time, questions about techniques or interpretations can be marked in pencil in the margins. The report may serve as an agenda for the next scheduled individual research conference. The monthly research report also serves as a training tool. It may suggest alternative explanations and presentations of data. It will no doubt offer lessons in spelling, punctuation, and referencing skills.

In addition to individual and small group conferences,

gatherings of the entire research group should be planned each semester or quarter. These meetings can be scheduled every two or three weeks and they should provide opportunities for researchers to present current findings or to give mock presentations in preparation for national or regional professional meetings. Newly enlisted researchers should be asked to give a talk about their previous accomplishments if they already have an earned degree. This talk could be followed a few weeks later by a presentation carefully outlining their current research program. This encourages the novice to thoroughly review background information for what might be a newly initiated area of research.

I schedule research-group meetings to last about one and one-half hours. Preliminary remarks by the research manager can be made to inform the group of certain upcoming events (e.g., a forthcoming national meeting or a visitor scheduled to speak). Announcements are followed by a 45- to-50-minute talk and, finally, by a question-and-answer period. Several times during the year, the research manager encourages researchers to ask questions during research-group meetings and to minimize inhibition arising from possible feelings of inadequate knowledge. A spirit of *understanding* and *courtesy* should be fostered so that everyone benefits from the research-group meeting. It is useful for the research manager to schedule himself/herself for a talk at research group meetings about once or twice during the year. This bolsters moral (see Chapter 7) and serves as a model for researchers.

The organized research-group meetings should emphasize the sense of accountability which researchers must develop toward society. Research efforts are, after all, most often supported by the state or federal government. These meetings also help researchers to organize, prepare, and deliver talks—tasks which they will have to perform many times during their careers. Such experience is invaluable for any researcher who eventually expects to deliver talks before national groups.

Research-group meetings provide a formal means of keeping all members of the research team informed concerning the pursuits of the group. This will serve as a stimulus for researchers to keep abreast of the literature. This overview also allows those who may not be intimately involved in a project to make suggestions and recommend remedies for described difficulties. Frequently, insights which may have eluded those close to a problem will be provided by individuals further removed and shared with the team.

7

Boosting Morale and Providing Encouragement

Most, if not all, university-based research managers will regularly be working with students or technicians who are new to research and with postdoctoral fellows who will be new to the research group. Since research involves many disappointments and failures, new recruits will, no doubt, experience considerable stress during their first few months.

In addition to the uncertainty posed by new rules and new environments, the beginning researchers' problems are generally compounded by poor to marginal salaries. Thus, the research manager is challenged by the need to generate the commitment from researchers that is required for keeping her/him in a competitive position for continuing grant-contract support. Fortunately, the research manager holds a trump card. Research can be enjoyable! Indeed, few human activities are as personally satisfying as those associated with discovery. Moreover, accomplishments in research are self-reflexive, creating even greater and more frequent accomplishments. This is the message a research manager can give to the novice researcher: "success leads to success," and "research leads to more research and greater satisfaction."

I find that there is a reluctance on the part of new graduate students to perform research. This is quite possibly due to their initial failures in the laboratory or to a general "fear of the unknown." Indeed, until the students accomplish something of worth, there may be frequent crises of incentive. It is useful, therefore, to suggest to students that their dedication is particularly necessary at first to achieve some measure of success later. Once they have a satisfying accomplishment or two behind them, future research efforts (even with the unavoidable, occasional failure) can be faced more optimistically. I frequently counsel students, telling them that after they have reached a certain stage of accomplishment then, and only then, will they be able to begin each day with the thought, "even if everything goes wrong today, I have something to fall back on." This feeling of confidence enables the researchers to apply themselves even more effectively; and, inevitably, other successful experiments will follow, giving the researcher greater and greater personal rewards.

To sustain researchers' motivation, the research manager must use wit as well as wisdom. The experienced researcher can appreciate the humor embodied in the aphorism commonly known as Murphy's Law: "If anything can go wrong, it will!" However, he/she knows that good ideas in a matrix of persistence often lead to real success.

An important attribute of the research manager alluded to earlier is accessibility. Both the appearance and the fact of accessibility may be achieved, in part, by leaving the office door wide open and by encouraging researchers to bring their concerns to one's attention at any time. The effective research manager should also determine to visit the laboratories several times each day. When the research group is very small (two or three persons), the research manager often can personally conduct experiments with the students. As a group expands, this becomes less possible; however, the need for laboratory contact does not diminish. Indeed, many new researchers will feel too inhibited to come to the research manager's office. If the research manager is available in the laboratory daily, he/she is more apt to hear their questions and concerns.

The research manager must also show sincere concern for the personal and professional needs of the researchers. This may be expressed through interested inquiries about the health of the researcher, for example. Also, it is important to keep researchers aware of university benefits (e.g., changes in health insurance coverage) and personal opportunities (e.g., job opportunities for graduating students).

University policies vary concerning merit raises. If these are possible, they can provide an excellent boost in researchers' morale. In addition to the merit increase, which may amount to only thirty to fifty dollars a month, there can be an even greater benefit if the research manager writes a letter to the employee documenting the reasons for the increase. This letter becomes part of the researcher's personal file and may be used as reference material in preparing letters of recommendation later on.

Mechanisms which may be used to foster mutual inspiration among researchers were covered earlier in descriptions of format and procedures for research-group meetings. The importance of meetings cannot be underestimated. Indeed, if one accepts the concept of "a critical mass" that helps to make positive results self-sustaining, then further means of promoting communication should be of great interest to the research manager.

One good mechanism for getting researchers together is the formation of a "journal club." This can be formulated somewhat informally and based on one-hour gatherings every one or two weeks in which single journal articles pertinent to all participating members are discussed. The group should have a leader at each meeting, who has the assignment of studying an article in some depth. Journal-club meetings can be scheduled during lunch-hour periods and people can be encouraged to bring a "bag lunch." This helps to keep the meetings low-keyed and promotes the spirit of learning while the group enjoys the simple physical pleasure of eating.

I have discovered a number of devices which have proven useful in improving communication between researchers. One such device is to see that preprints of manuscripts prepared by any member(s) of the group are distributed to all researchers. This sharing is likewise recommended for grant proposals. Memo boxes or file trays labeled with the name of each researcher may be maintained for distribution purposes in the research manager's office area. These boxes become an information depository which researchers are encouraged to check regularly. In the process of picking up the mail, researchers will come into contact with the research manager and be encouraged to ask questions or comment on their most recent research findings.

The research manager should also prepare routing slips to be attached to materials which are of general interest and which should be passed along from researcher to researcher. The research manager may also wish to disseminate current awareness publications, such as *Current Contents*, in this way. I provide student researchers with preaddressed reprint request cards available through the Institute of Scientific Information. Individual researchers initial the return address labels of these cards as they are sent out so that returned reprints can be properly routed.

An effective research manager is likely to be asked to review several manuscripts and books for journals during the year. These opportunities can be used to train students to effectively and constructively criticize the work of others. It is difficult to involve more than one student in any given review; however, this may be a good one-to-one exercise between the researcher and the research manager. After the review is complete, appropriate acknowledgment of the student's contribution is forwarded to the editor who requested the review. I have used this procedure many times to gain co-authorship for students on published book reviews and to enlist students as independent reviewers of journals.

Social gatherings hosted by the research manager greatly enhance communication and instill camaraderie within the research group. These affairs need not be fancy; an afternoon picnic or an evening party held in connection with the visit of a professor from another university are both quite suitable. I usually invite one or more professorial friends from allied departments at the university, thus providing an excellent forum for exchange of ideas between individuals who are not accessible to each other on a day-to-day basis.

8

Needs of Different Types of Personnel

Different researchers have different needs. The research manager will have to develop unique relationships with technicians, undergraduate researchers, graduate students, and postdoctoral associates in accordance with those needs.

Technicians are usually employed when there is considerable routine work to do. For example, a given project may require chemical analysis of several hundred samples. Thus, the technician will have to be motivated to perform some rather tedious tasks. At the same time, a sense of carefulness must be imbued in the technician so that the data collected from earlier samples in the study are as reliable as the data from later samples. While the research manager continually emphasizes the need for care in the generation of data, the technician must have some sense of independence and a feeling of responsibility. This is partly achieved by establishing quality control and preventive maintenance routines in a technician's work schedule. Certain indications of instrumental or reagent failure may be described for the technician, and he/she then may be shown the remedies for such problems. Thus, the technician can make independent judgments while performing routine tasks.

Technicians can be given certain procurement responsibilities and held accountable for shortages which may be clearly due to poor planning. Again, a certain amount of responsibility makes technicians' jobs more interesting and places technicians in the position of making individual contributions to the group's effort.

The research manager will find it useful to meet with technicians weekly. Also, technicians can be invited to research-group meetings if they express sincere interest in projects being pursued by the researchers. Occasionally, bachelor-level technicians may decide to pursue graduate work under one's direction. It has been my experience that many bright and formerly unmotivated people at this level follow this course of action. Thus, the extra time and effort spent with a technician can occasionally provide added benefits.

Undergraduate researchers present some interesting challenges for the research manager. The undergradute researcher is usually registered for ten or more course hours and, therefore, has extensive classroom commitments. She/he may be hired on a part-time basis (typically ten to twenty hours) or may register for a research projects course under your direction. In either case, conscientious effort and time commitment should be demanded from undergraduate researchers. If they are taking a three-semester-hours, research projects course, it should be expected that they will spend a minimum of nine hours per week in the laboratory. Sometimes this formula (i.e., course hours times three) is mandated by the university. It should be emphasized to the undergraduate researcher that the nine-hour commitment (or its equivalent for courses with lower or higher semester-hour assignments) is a minimum requirement. Additional hours should be devoted to the research program for optimum results.

Once the number of hours has been agreed upon, the undergraduate researcher should supply the research manager with a schedule outlining the days and periods that he/she intends to work in the laboratory. This will help the research manager to better plan laboratory contact with the undergraduate researcher.

The undergraduate researcher is frequently naïve about research methodology and laboratory technique. She/he will require close supervision, especially during the first month or so in the laboratory. Consequently, the research manager may find it useful to assign the undergraduate researcher to a senior graduate student or a postdoctoral fellow. When possible, the undergraduate will attend scheduled conferences planned by the research manager and the undergraduate's laboratory supervisor.

Plans for experiments should consider the special needs of the undergraduate, for example, exposing the individual to a variety of techniques and equipment.

In the best of cases, the undergraduate researcher will grow more proficient as the quarter or semester progresses, and more independent experiments can be assigned. Because of the limited time commitment of undergraduate researchers, I require only one research report (at the end of the academic unit), but this report should be as thorough and professional as those required of graduate students and postdoctoral researchers (see Chapter 6).

The undergraduate researcher is encouraged to attend and participate in research-group meetings. Indeed, these individuals can be scheduled to give one presentation toward the end of their semester (quarter) in residence.

The undergraduate student, like other researchers in the group, should have a desk in the laboratory. She/he may be encouraged to utilize the laboratory as a place to study during those times when there are no experiments scheduled. Actually, this fringe benefit serves as a good incentive for undergraduates to enroll in the research projects courses. However, the undergraduate should be advised that this privilege is only extended to him/her. The laboratory should not be turned into a study hall for groups of undergraduates. As a general rule, the research manager should consistently promote the idea that the laboratory is a place for active experimentation, data analysis, and discussion of research.

Graduate students may be the backbone of the research group. They also present some unique challenges to research managers. This is true because a graduate student (particularly a predoctoral student) may be associated with the research group for a period of four years or longer. During this time, graduate students face the normal problems of personal maturing. They may be newly married. Frequently they have financial difficulties. Finally, and of no small importance, they will have recently undergone the transition from undergraduate to graduate studies and will be tackling some of the most difficult work (course and otherwise) they have ever encountered.

Every effort should be made by the research manager to convince the graduate students (particularly the novices) that research is the most important part of their program. This is necessary to meet the dissertation requirements for Ph.D. students and to sustain the viability of the research manager's program, as noted earlier (Chapter 6). Graduate students have a tendency to put aside research when course demands become heavy, for example, when examinations are being given and term papers are due. Nevertheless, the research manager must place emphasis on continual research efforts. While research activity may occasionally diminish, it should not be halted even though the students are preparing for other academic tasks. In fact, developing the habit of doing two or more things at once is excellent training for the students' future career.

I often admonish student researchers to "make things count double!" This means that one should integrate activities which may serve two or more purposes. Indeed, this approach is necessary in making research assignments for graduate students. The students need projects which will be valuable in preparation of their dissertation or thesis requirements. In addition, the objectives of the research manager's research program must be met. One approach is to initially assign a graduate student to a project which is only part of a larger problem (see also Chapter 10). This smaller project is carefully chosen for its likelihood of success. As mentioned earlier (Chapter 7), the novice researcher needs success in the early phases of his/her work to help build the confidence necessary to tackle larger and more complex problems.

The above recommendations should not be mis-construed. A good research manager has no illusions about the difficulty of research. Anything that is worth doing and worth supporting may very well be difficult. To explicate this, I frequently tell students that "all the easy problems have been solved!"

Graduate student researchers are somewhat unusual members of a research team because they face demands posed by a number of groups within the institution. They must meet course requirements and participate in depart-mental or college-wide seminars. They have to pass qualify-ing and preliminary examinations. The research manager should always be aware of these demands and take some time during individual research conferences (see Chapter 6) to inquire about relevant problems.

Counseling of predoctoral students is particularly impor-tant prior to preliminary or comprehensive examinations. The research manager should empathize with the anxiety that students experience during this period and should be somewhat lenient regarding expectations for research pro-ductivity during the time preceding such a major examina-tion. It is my experience that a reasonable time for the intensive study required for a comprehensive examination is about one month.

Graduate students can be supported financially by teaching assistantships or research assistantships, which may be funded by the university or, most often in the latter case, through grant/contract funds. I seek support for graduate students through teaching assistantships for the first year or two. After this, research assistantship funds should be ob-

tained so that students can devote maximum effort to their research. Regardless of funding and its associated require-ments (e.g., laboratory teaching responsibilities in the case of a teaching assistantship), graduate student researchers should recognize their research commitments for as long as they are a part of the research group.

Postdoctoral students are the most important members of the university research group, and research managers can expect the greatest contributions from these individuals. These contributions do not come without planning and se-rious administrative effort, however. The research manager must recruit the best available postdoctoral fellows (Chapter 2). After proper orientation (Chapter 5), a research program is developed for the postdoctoral researcher. I typically assign two problems or research areas to every postdoctoral fellow. One problem will have short-term goals which may lead to rapid results, while the second will be more demanding and will have longer-range objectives.

Since the postdoctoral researcher is the senior (in experience, if not in age) member of your research team, a certain amount of leadership ability is expected of her/him. The postdoctoral student should serve as the laboratory's "model researcher" and should be required to take extra care in laboratory technique. Undergraduates, graduate students, and technicians need to feel comfortable in discussing everyday laboratory problems with the postdoctoral researcher. The research manager should make it clear that he/she expects the postdoctoral person to assume some responsibility for the overall welfare of the research team.

Because of their responsible status, the research manager should have a special relationship with postdoctoral researchers. These persons are truly colleagues, and the research manager should treat them as such. It is to be expected in time that the postdoctoral researcher will contribute more and more ideas to the overall research program. In a way, he/she may also become a confidant(e) and advisor. This type of relationship prepares postdoctoral students for the permanent positions in which they will need to interact with other doctoral-level people.

While postdoctoral researchers are exclusively accountable to the research manager, they nevertheless need to have a sense of common purpose with the college, department, or research institute. The research manager should feel perfectly free to ask a postdoctoral associate to present a department-wide seminar or to give an occasional lecture in an undergraduate or graduate course. These efforts enrich the research manager's academic unit.

An effective postdoctoral researcher with excellent ideas can be encouraged to seek independent funding. He/she may apply for a postdoctoral fellowship (see Chapter 1) or become the principal investigator on a grant of her/his own design. If the latter effort is successful and full salary support is generated, the possibility may exist for obtaining a faculty appointment for the postdoctoral fellow. An outstanding start in an academic career can thus be provided for this individual.

When possible, the research manager should reward postdoctoral researchers with appropriate raises. Fringe benefits, such as support for travel to at least one national meeting per year (see Chapter 9), should be provided. Postdoctoral researchers also should receive appropriate recognition for papers presented at meetings and publications in journals (see Chapter 10).

9

Travel Policies

New researchers need to attend professional meetings in order to see the caliber and types of work presented and to meet colleagues from other institutions. All researchers should be supported for travel to at least one professional meeting per year.

This opportunity, however, is frequently affected by budget restraints. Travel costs can be minimized by having a group drive to a regional meeting. For subsequent meetings, I follow the policy that researchers must be scheduled to present a paper to be funded for travel. Submittal of abstracts for meetings has to be coordinated with the research manager so that funding can be planned. In addition to travel funds available through research grants, departments and the graduate colleges may supply partial support for student travel. The student should investigate these sources, with the research manager's approval. Another possibility for funds is for graduate students and postdoctoral fellows to combine a job-interview trip with a professional meeting, allowing the interviewing agency to partially support travel to the meeting.

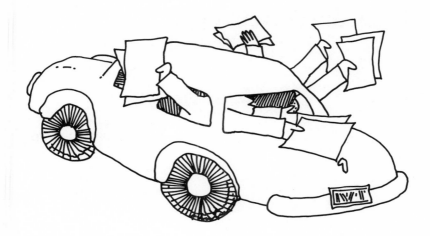

Researchers should know which documentation is necessary for travel to be considered official university business. Researchers should also be instructed in the preparation of appropriate justifications which may have to be submitted to superiors prior to approval for a trip. The researcher should also clearly understand which expenses are legal and proper for reimbursement.

After returning from a professional meeting, the research manager may want to ask the researcher to summarize the important papers. If this is planned prior to the trip, the research manager can suggest that such a summary be organized for presentation at a forthcoming research-group meeting.

10

Publication Activities

The publication of scholarly works serves the twofold purpose of reporting new experimental results and confirming those previously published. One cannot justify publishing the latter if this confirmation has been done too many times. There is, however, a place for some replication in the literature. This is especially true of studies where some repetition of previously published work is necessary to extend a given area of investigation.

The research manager must make decisions about which papers to publish, as well as when and where to publish them. As far as timing is concerned, it is important for the research manager to identify self-contained segments within larger projects which may merit publication. For example, a study of the disposition of a drug in animals will likely begin with experiments on methods for quantifying the drug in various tissues (e.g., blood serum, brain, liver, etc.). If a procedure is devised which exhibits definite advantages (e.g., improved sensitivity) over previously reported methods, then a paper on the procedure merits publication in a suitable journal.

Many journals publish several types of papers, including reviews, research articles or reports, notes, and communications. Reviews, as the name implies, provide an overview of the literature in a specific area. Authors should determine how definitive their review should be for any given publication. Some journals prefer exhaustive coverage, while others seek shorter, more timely reviews. Research managers should periodically prepare reviews in areas close to their own major research interests. This review provides incentive to carefully survey the works of others and also provides the opportunity to present a review of one's own work in a single paper. Thereby, the scientific community can evaluate the overall contribution of one's group in the context of the work of other researchers.

Research articles or reports describe definitive studies of substantial length, while notes present the results of investigations of lesser scope. Communications are reserved for work of greatest significance and generally are shortest in length. A communication may preceed the publication of a full-length research article. The research manager of a dynamic and productive group will have opportunities to publish all types of scientific papers. It is up to the research manager to decide which type is most appropriate for a given set of circumstances.

A journal is chosen after considering a number of factors, including appropriateness of the work being submitted, quality and readership of the journal, and cost (i.e., submittal fees and page charges) to the research group. Research managers who direct groups in rather narrow areas of study will generally favor a small selection of journals. Those who perform multidisciplinary or interdisciplinary work will have much broader options. A review of appropriate issues of *Current Comments*, or comparable current awareness pub-

lications, provides many titles of journals which can be used as an outlet for one's work. Research managers will, no doubt, have different formulas for choosing a journal. Generally, it is true that journals by the major scientific societies in the United States and many European countries are of the highest quality. Journals of lesser prestige which use a referee system to screen and evaluate submitted manuscripts are a good second choice. If one is performing studies outside his/her own field, as occurs often in multi- and inter-disciplinary work, the best "check" on the quality of one's efforts is to attempt publication of appropriate segments in highly respected, disciplinary journals.

The readership of a particular journal should be taken into account. If, for example, one wants to have his/her work read by the widest group of fellow authors, then a journal like *Science* (published by the American Association for the Advancement of Sciences) might be considered most appropriate. At other times, one may wish recognition from smaller bodies of scientists, and journals with more restricted readership will be suitable.

The actual preparation of an article must be done with great care. In general, authors' names are assigned to a paper according to their contribution. People should not be included in the authorship of a paper unless they have contributed to the studies it represents in some meaningful way. Frequently, the actual writing effort will fall upon the shoulders of the research manager. This serves the purpose of having her/him become more intimately acquainted with the work. It is often desirable to have senior graduate students or postdoctoral fellows prepare initial, if not final, drafts of papers. Revisions go back and forth between researchers and research manager until a mutually acceptable draft results. The final draft is most carefully typed. Beyond the very first draft, it is imperative that directions to authors prescribed by the journal on format and style are precisely followed.

Every article should have a primary author, and a first-position assignment is becoming more accepted as a position for the most important contributor. In some cases this will be the research manager, while in others a member of the research team will serve this capacity. The primary author should be designated principally responsible for returned manuscripts which may require alterations before publication. This person may also be charged with review and return of galley proofs.

The research manager must decide how many reprints are necessary to fill reprint requests. Sufficient numbers of reprints should be ordered to supply the needs of the research group over the next several years. Also, funding agencies frequently request multiple reprints of articles resulting from grants or contracts. After publication, the research manager should be in charge of providing reprints requested by researchers outside one's group. A procedure can be established with one's secretary to accomplish this task (see Chapters 4 and 13).

11

Purchasing Activities

When the research manager is principal investigator on grants and contracts he/she is ultimately responsible and accountable for expenditures of funds. Much of the daily ordering and purchasing of supplies and equipment, however, should be delegated to researchers. Typed requests are submitted to the research manager for written approval. This presents an opportunity to ask questions about the requested items.

After getting approval, the researcher forwards the purchase order request to the purchasing agent. The researcher should retain a copy of the initial request and record the purchase order number unless university procedure dictates that this number be assigned later. When this is the case, the researcher should be informed of the number assigned so that tracers can be issued in cases of delayed or mislaid orders. In my institute an initiator's copy of the order, complete with purchase order number, is forwarded to the researcher soon after the order has been sent to a vendor.

A system of inventory control can be instituted in the research manager's laboratory for chemicals and research supplies. Responsibility for the system can be assigned to a technician or other individual who would be charged with listing items on index cards and keeping track of usage by frequent checks of the cards, which should be kept alphabetically in a file box. Such an inventory system requires the cooperation of all researchers, who should be admonished to register usage of items listed in the inventory file.

Procedural manuals for ordering supplies and equipment should be available in the researcher's laboratory. Research managers should continually remind researchers that purchasing agents and business staff members strictly adhere to establishment business practices. Thus, they will not be willing to break the rules to expedite receipt of a needed chemical or piece of apparatus. There are usually mechanisms for processing emergency orders, and these must be used judiciously.

Researchers need an occasional reminder that university staff, whether in an accounting office or other service support group, have no vested interest in research and tend to act dispassionately toward expressed needs in research missions. The best advice to the researcher is to be courteous but persistent. A harried staff member may occasionally pass a request on to someone else merely to be rid of it. The researcher must persist in explaining her/his need until a satisfactory answer to a problem is obtained.

The research manager should receive a monthly printout of all research accounts. Ideally, expenditures and encumbrances should be itemized, with free balances shown in each category (i.e., salaries and wages, supplies, equipment, and travel). If this service is not available through the university business manager's office, such a service should be instituted through a departmental or collegiate business officer. Care should be exercised in shifting moneys from one expense category to another to accommodate priority changes or unintentional overdrafts. The research manager should check on the legality of such transfers with the sponsored projects office or directly with the granting agency.

Most research managers will have teaching obligations in their university which involve laboratory courses. If there are experiments in these courses which can be related to one's research, then the research manager can benefit in two ways. First, the experiments will be more readily implemented and debugged because of a familiarity with underlying principles and procedures. Second, supplies left over from the laboratory courses may be used in research when it is not practical to store them for a future semester. Equipment used in the course will often be free for sufficient periods of time to be used in research. The effective research manager should always watch for situations like this which may help him/her to "make things count double!"

12

Maintenance and Operation of Equipment

Research in the physical, chemical, and biological sciences requires an array of sophisticated electronic equipment, maintenance of which can be costly. Thus, it is important for the research manager to have policies regarding equipment usage and upkeep.

Frequently, one member of the research team will be more mechanically or electronically adept than others. A research manager who is aware of this talent may try to encourage this researcher to assume responsibility for helping the others with equipment use and troubleshooting. Other researchers with unique talents should be asked to make general contributions to the group (e.g., the researcher with keen ability in statistics). The researcher identified as instrumentation specialist can be charged with minor preventive maintenance routines and liaison work with companies which may need to be contacted for equipment repair.

Every laboratory should have an assortment of high-quality tools. Loaning these tools to other groups should be discouraged. All tools should be inscribed with the lab number and the research manager's name or initials. Serious attempts to repair equipment should be encouraged and supported. Soldering, tap and die work, and construction of small parts and components are services which can frequently be obtained from university machine and electrical shops. These groups can thus be a source of significant cost savings.

Often, equipment malfunctions result from carelessness or improper handling. A researcher in the group (perhaps the instrumentation specialist) can be charged with teaching instrument operation to new researchers. A more efficient approach is to compile written standard operating procedures (SOP's) for all equipment used by the group. The SOP's can be prepared by researchers as part of a laboratory techniques course and posted close to the equipment. SOP's for frequently used laboratory procedures can also be similarly posted, as indicated in Chapter 6.

13

Maintenance of Literature Files and References

With the advent of current awareness publications, ready photocopying services, and the great proliferation of journals in recent years, there is a growing trend toward the collection of reprints of scientific articles for literature referrals. I have devised a method for the storing and use of reprints which is easily adapted, requires no special equipment or supplies, can readily be maintained by secretarial help, and is easily used by researchers.

Reprint cards available from the Institute for Scientific Information can be used in such a way as to keep a record of reprints requested and received. This task can be delegated entirely to the research manager's secretary. Appropriate descriptors are assigned to reprints which have been received and perused. The descriptors are printed in the upper right-hand corner of the front page of the reprint and one of these is designated primary descriptor by two underlines. The reprint is then stamped with the word *index* in the upper left-hand corner and placed in a file box for the secretary's attention. The secretary types a 3" x 5" card for the primary descriptor and lists the full reference citation. Cards with secondary descriptors are cross-referenced to the primary descriptor. All index cards and the reprints are filed alphabetically in two separate file cabinets. Special research interests will cause the research manager to collect many reprints which have the same primary descriptor. These can be subfiled chronologically. After file cards are prepared, the word *index* is struck from the front page of the indexed reprint and replaced with the word *file*. After being subsequently retrieved and used, the reprint can be placed in a file box for return to the reprint file. The new "file" notation prevents confusion as to whether indexing or filing is required of the secretary.

In addition to the index-card procedure and reprint file, a system has been devised by me for correlating recent literature reports with currently pursued research projects. Research managers usually have a research proposal associated with each major investigation being pursued in her/his laboratory. These documents typically have twenty or more pages. The proposal can be properly punched and placed in a looseleaf binder. As reprints of articles are received which have relevance to a working project, notation is made in the proposal binder. This can be accomplished by penciling-in a number at a given place in the proposal and typing an explanation on an adjacent page in the binder. In the explanation, the principal descriptor is provided, which will permit easy retrieval of the original article from the reprint file. This system has two advantages. First, it encourages the research manager to continually review the funded proposal; this is a good reminder of objectives and recommendations originally made for experiments. Second, the resulting annotated proposal will be of great benefit in preparing yearly (or quarterly) reports and competitive renewal applications.

14

Secretarial and Support Staff

Researchers often exhibit two types of behavior which are detrimental to good relationships with secretaries and other staff members. Some researchers, because of their position, may consider themselves superior to staff personnel. Others, who are very enthusiastic about their research, may be disappointed when staff members do not feel similar excitement.

The research manager may have to remind researchers that staff members have their own interests and goals and may not always respond as anticipated to researchers' needs. A good research manager strives to impress upon staff members that the mission of her/his research group is important. These people should be especially aware of the need to expend public funds in the most efficient way possible.

Staff members, naturally, wish to be treated politely and in a cheerful way. They need clear and careful directions in order to accomplish assigned work. Student researchers, who are sometimes not sufficiently mature to handle the pressures placed on them, need occasional reminders along these lines.

Efficient and loyal staff members are invaluable to the

research manager, who can increase productivity severalfold through these people by proper delegation of responsibilities and by inspiring a sense of carefulness in the performance of their duties.

The research manager must find ways to cut time spent on routine administrative tasks (see Chapter 16). A secretary who can take accurate dictation is a great help. Secretaries should also handle most filing, mailing operations, and travel arrangements.

A senior secretary or administrative assistant can prepare appointment forms, assist with purchasing procedures, and keep necessary personnel records. This individual may also take part in budget preparations and analyses. Some secretarial staff persons may have unique talents, such as the ability to help with editorial work, which can be most useful to the research manager. He/she should develop the attitude that there is no disgrace connected with delegating any work which can be satisfactorily performed by a staff person.

In addition to secretarial help, the research manager may want to hire work-study people each semester (quarter) to help with routine tasks (e.g., washing glassware) and to serve as "go-fors" in the office. Federal work-study programs provide 80 percent contributions to the salary of students who work in this capacity. For an investment of a few hundred dollars per semester (quarter), help can be obtained which can free researchers and the research manager from many essentially nonproductive laboratory and office tasks. I also use work-study people to scan the *Commerce Business Daily* for notices of interest to the research program. To aid in this assignment, the work-study individual is given a complete list of descriptors which are used to earmark potentially interesting notices and bring them to my attention. RFP's of interest are subsequently requested (see Chapter 1).

15

Public Relations Activities

A professor once said, "If you can't explain your research to just anyone, you don't understand it yourself!" And, yet, research managers often feel hard-pressed to describe their research in laymen's terms. Science, clearly, is ill-understood by most of society. This is unfortunate, even in the best of times. Now, there is a strong need for greater input from the scientific community to solve the complex problems we are currently facing. Society's present mood of frugality makes it more important than ever to explain carefully the reasons for continued tax support of research activities, particularly since the support of research and development by industry has declined in recent years. For these reasons, alone, it should be evident that public relations are quite important and that time should be devoted to educating the public about the research missions and activities of the group.

Most universities have news and information bureaus with staff journalists to help with these efforts. Newsworthy discoveries and results need to be brought to the attention of these individuals regularly. The research manager should not

attempt to prepare copy. Rather, he/she should notify the news and information group and they will usually cooperate in preparing a story suitable for dissemination to lay publications and trade journals. The news and information group should be informed when the research manager or a member of the group is honored by a scientific organization or scholarly institution. This benefits the entire research team and gains the attention of colleagues all across campus. Occasionally, a colleague on campus with similar interests may first become aware of the group's activities through articles or reports appearing in a campus publication. This may lead to worthwhile collaborative efforts.

Some universities publish magazines which describe the research endeavors of various groups on campus. An opportunity to contribute an article to such a publication should be actively pursued, for this recognition boosts the morale of the research team. Also, the resulting article may be used in two ways. First, it can be helpful in recruiting new graduate students or undergraduate researchers who might experience difficulty in understanding the research effort merely by reading technical articles. Second, many grant proposals, particularly those submitted to foundations (see Chapter 1), will require laymen's summaries, which can be readily constructed from this sort of article.

A word of warning, however, concerning the public relations function is in order. Occasionally one may be misunderstood by news and information people. It is therefore imperative that any copy prepared for public consumption be approved by the research manager in advance of publication.

16

Time Management

Time management is the answer to the question, "Where do I find the time to implement the ideas put forth in the preceding chapters?" Alan Lakein has outlined helpful time-use systems in his recent book on the subject of time management (see Bibliography), and I have been able to adapt several of these systems to the particular needs of the research manager—academician.

A "to-do" list can be a valuable tool which will serve as a reminder of tasks which require attention. This list may be no more than a legal pad on which to jot down, for example, that paper X is to be written, researcher Y's report needs to be read, student Z wants a letter of recommendation, and so on. As jobs are completed, they are crossed off the list and new ones added as necessary.

Lakein recommends that items on the list be assigned priorities: A, B, and C. Suborder priorities are designated by numerical notations: 1,2, 3. The highest priority tasks are A-1's. Lakein admonishes his readers to concentrate their efforts on A's. He postulates the 80/20 rule, which promises the success of any program (80% of it, anyway, will be

accomplished upon the effective completion of 20% of the
A's on the "to-do" list). I use such a list daily and find it
extremely helpful. The list should become a permanent fix-
ture on the research manager's desk.

In addition to the "to-do" list, I use a monthly calendar
book to outline necessary daily activities. The calendar book
is placed in an open position on the far right-hand corner of
my desk. This book is a schema for accomplishing the many
tasks which occupy the research manager's day.

Highest priority is given to teaching and research obligations. Time wasted in the discharge of one of these activities,

obviously, takes time away from the other. For this reason, the research manager should develop mechanisms for improving efficiency where possible. For example, in teaching, preparing notes, audiovisual aids, and handouts well in advance will improve effectiveness of the research manager during the semester or quarter a course is given. I usually take about a month to accomplish this for a new course. During this time much effort is given to polishing the quality of lectures, which will help to eliminate confusion on the part of students during class and minimize the necessity for after-class contact. Another way to help in this respect is to begin each lecture session with a question period and to encourage students to question during lectures. The adequate preparation for a course will mean the difference between having and not having time for research or other important work while the course is being taught.

Appointments with researchers and students will, no doubt, occupy a significant portion of the day's time, and students should be welcomed to the office in a friendly manner, but they must know that the research manager is not interested in frivolous conversations (meetings with researchers are discussed in more detail in Chapter 6). A great deal of time will be saved by establishing such a posture. Earlier it was recommended that researchers be prompted to visit the office at any time. During encounters with researchers, just as with students, the attempt must be made to keep discussion businesslike.

The monthly calendar book should be used for scheduling appointments of all kinds. The research manager's secretary can be encouraged to consult the calendar for scheduling when necessary.

I also use a calendar pad, which is located on my desk, to make notes for follow-up calls, short memos, personal reminders, reminders of materials to be brought from home to work or vice versa, and so forth. The practice of writing notes to oneself is also helpful.

Another time-saving tool can be developed by surveying the notes most often sent back and forth between the research manager and her/his secretary. These notes, such as "Please make copies of this paper," can be prepared in bulk and thereby save the time of writing them out.

Every moment saved represents time put to better use. Lakein recommends that people establish the habit of asking themselves, "What is the best use of my time right now?" This may be the first step toward becoming more conscious of time and its value.

Summary of Guidelines
for Developing and Managing
Research Groups

Summary of Guidelines

Below is a list of highlights taken from the text. The reader may wish to scan these periodically to refresh her/his memory. This list can also be effectively used by research managers to prepare lectures for research group meetings or seminars (see Chapter 6).

Developing the Research Group

1. Obtaining Grant Support
   - Accountability in the expenditure of free gifts and grant and contract funds is a necessity.
   - Grants and contracts have varying degrees of flexibility.
   - Scan the *Commerce Business Daily* for relevant RFP's.
   - Bidding on contracts can be rigorous.
   - Encourage predoctorals and postdoctorals to apply for fellowships.
   - Develop relationships with co-investigators very carefully.

- Describe collaborative work in grant proposals as thoroughly as possible.
- Flexibility and imagination help motivate mission-oriented research.
- Prepare written inquiries to foundations and industrial firms before sending the formal grant proposal.
- Develop a standard format for grant proposals.
- Emphasize the preparation of effective grant summaries (abstracts).
- Develop budget preparation guidelines.
- Do not forget the relative importance of biographical sketches and appendices of grant proposals.

2. Recruiting Personnel
   - Recent baccalaureate graduates make good technical help.
   - Recruit graduate students on your own.
   - Develop a protocol for recruiting postdoctoral students.
   - Use the telephone to get references on postdoctoral students.
   - Develop a format for offering positions to postdoctoral fellows which includes job descriptions and information on university and locale.
   - Prepare and maintain a recruitment file.
   - Help the new postdoctoral associate relocate.

3. Procuring Equipment and Instrumentation Services
   - "Permanent equipment" costs more than $1,000.
   - Obtain the proper approval for budget changes to purchase permanent equipment.
   - Federal programs to purchase permanent equipment are available.
   - Purchase equipment which can benefit both teaching and research mission.

- Surplus equipment is available to NSF grantees.
- Acquisition of equipment jointly with other departments and institutions should be carefully planned.
- Establish and maintain a "desired equipment" file for quick processing of purchase requests.
- Investigate university-wide equipment sources which may be supported through overhead or other grant-related funds.
4. Developing Collaborative Arrangements
   - One's research reputation encourages extramural collaborative arrangements.
   - Communication is needed for successful research collaboration.

Managing the Research Group

5. Orientation of Personnel
   - Formal orientation sessions serve all researchers.
   - The first orientation session should offer logistical information and an introduction to research goals.
   - Establish and maintain a personal information file.
   - Develop "personal" and "research" file folders for each new researcher.
   - The second orientation session should cover reporting requirements and the design of initial experiments.
6. Reporting Mechanisms
   - Plan individual and research-group conferences and meetings every semester or quarter.
   - Schedule weekly or bi-weekly individual research conferences.

- Plan special joint meetings of researchers in inter-disciplinary work on an ad hoc basis.
- Require monthly research reports from all researchers, except undergraduates.
- Monthly research reports should be prepared in the style of journal articles.
- Encourage the development of appendices to monthly reports which describe frequently used experimental routines.
- Use monthly reports as a training tool.
- Research managers should occasionally present talks in research-group meetings.

7. Boosting Morale and Providing Encouragement
   - Empathize with new researcher's problems and frustrations.
   - Develop positive attitudes toward research based on the paradigm, "Research is enjoyable and accomplishments are self-reflexive."
   - Be accessible and show concern for the personal welfare of researchers.
   - Do not neglect daily laboratory visits.
   - Provide merit raises when possible.
   - Develop journal clubs.
   - Distribute internally developed manuscripts and grant proposals to all researchers for comments.
   - Share materials of general interest with the research group.
   - Have researchers aid in the review of manuscripts and books.
   - Plan occasional social gatherings for the research group.

8. Needs of Different Types of Personnel

- Encourage technicians to exercise independent judgment.
- Explain the commitment required of undergraduate researchers and provide for daily supervision and varied laboratory experiences.
- Emphasize the importance of research in graduate students' programs but empathize with the demands placed on them by departments and other groups at the university.
- Develop two research problems with different goals for postdoctoral researchers.
- Postdoctoral researchers should assume leadership roles and contribute ideas to research projects.
- The postdoctoral researcher is a colleague who may become a confidant(e) and advisor.
- Expect some commitment from the postdoctoral student to the departmental or collegiate unit.
- Provide encouragement and help to postdoctoral researchers who try to obtain individual grant funding or fellowships.

9. Travel Policies
   - Encourage researchers to travel to professional meetings to present papers.
   - Obtain travel funds from the graduate school or by combining interview trips with attendance at professional meetings.
   - Researchers should be aware of the internal documentation needed for travel on official business.
   - Information gained at symposia can serve as the basis for presentations in research-group meetings.

10. Publication Activities
    - Identify segments of work which are suitable to be

published and determine in which journal publication will be sought.

- Seek out opportunities to prepare review articles which relate to the group's major research interest.
- A dynamic research group produces all types of publications.
- A primary author is assigned to each manuscript and is principally responsible for all processes leading to publication.

11. Purchasing Activities
    - Routine purchasing activities should be delegated to researchers and appropriate staff personnel.
    - Require researchers to keep copies of orders and record purchase order numbers.
    - Procedural manuals for ordering supplies and chemicals should be available in the laboratory.
    - Obtain and monitor all research account balances through monthly print-outs.
    - Combine teaching and research missions in the design of experiments and in the purchase of material for undergraduate laboratory courses.

12. Maintenance and Operation of Equipment
    - Appoint an instrumentation specialist in the laboratory.
    - Develop a tool collection and encourage researchers to make equipment repairs.
    - Use university electrical and machine shops when possible.
    - Post SOP's for all equipment in the laboratory near the apparatus.

13. Maintenance of Literature Files and References
    - Develop a literature filing system for reprints of scientific articles.

- Prepare binders for currently active research grants and devise an update system.
14. Secretarial and Support Staff
    - Promote good relations between support staff and researchers.
    - Foster special talents displayed by support staff.
    - Hire work-study staff persons for routine clerical and laboratory work.
15. Public Relations Activities
    - Take time for public relations efforts.
    - Work closely with university news and information bureaus.
    - Encourage invitations to prepare articles for the university's research magazine.
    - Read, modify as necessary, and approve any copy for public consumption.
16. Time Management
    - Prepare a "to-do" list and use it properly.
    - Use a monthly calendar book to help schedule and meet daily appointments.
    - Use a daily calendar pad for reminders and memos to oneself.
    - Minimize out-of-class contact time with students by careful preparation of course materials and effective use of class hours.
    - Establish a businesslike posture in dealings with students and researchers.
    - Continue to ask yourself, "What is the best use of my time right now?"

Bibliography

Benet, L. Z. "Obligations of a Major Professor to a Graduate Student." *Amer. J. Pharm. Educ.* 41 (1977): 383–385.

Cherim, S. M. *Chemistry for Laboratory Technicians*. Philadelphia: Saunders, 1970.

Day, R. A. *How to Write and Publish a Scientific Paper*. Philadelphia: ISI Press, 1979.

Ewing, D. W. *Writing for Results in Business, Government and the Professions*. New York: Wiley-Interscience, 1974.

Farnsworth, N. R. "Effective Management and Operation of Graduate Programs in Colleges of Pharmacy." *Amer. J. Pharm. Educ.* 41 (1977): 375–378.

Freedman, P. *The Principles of Scientific Research*. 2d ed. New York: Pergamon Press, 1960.

Gilman, H. "Some Aspects of Interdisciplinary Research." *Chem. Eng. News* 55, no. 13 (1977): 49–52.

Grants for Scientific Research (NSF 78–41). Washington, D.C.: National Science Foundation, 1978.

Guide to Health Grants and Contracts. New York: McGraw-Hill, 1978.

Guide to NIH Programs and Awards (NIH 76–33). Bethesda: National Institutes of Health, 1976.

Handbook for Authors of Papers in American Chemical Society

Bibliography

Publications. Washington D.C.: American Chemical Society, 1978.

Henley, C. "Peer Review of Research Grant Applications at the National Institutes of Health 1: The Assignment and Referral Processes." *Fed. Proc.* 36 (1977): 2066–2068.

——. "Peer Review of Research Grant Applications at the National Institutes of Health 2: Review by an Initial Review Group." *Fed. Proc.* 36 (1977): 2187–2190.

——. "Peer Review of Research Grant Applications at the National Institutes of Health 3: Review by an Advisory Board/Council." *Fed. Proc.* 36 (1977): 2335–2338.

Instruction Sheet, Rev. 2–73 for NIH 398. Bethesda: National Institutes of Health, 1977.

Lakein, A. *How to Get Control of Your Time and Your Life.* New York: Signet, 1973.

Merritt, D. H., and Eaves, G. N. "Site Visits for the Review of Grant Applications to the National Institutes of Health: Views of an Applicant and a Scientist Administrator." *Fed. Proc.* 34 (1975): 131–136.

O'Connor, M., and Woodford, F. P. *Writing Scientific Papers in English.* New York: Elsevier, 1977.

Overberger, C. G. "Universities and the Federal Government: A Marriage That Has Survived." *Chem. Eng. News* 56, no. 49 (1978): 28–30.

Pelz, D. C., and Andrews, F. M. *Scientists in Organizations: Productive Climates for Research and Development.* Rev. ed. Ann Arbor: Institute for Social Research, 1976.

Roy, R. "Interdisciplinary Science on Campus: The Elusive Dream." *Chem. Eng. News* 55, no. 35 (1977): 28–40.

Smith, R. V. "Good Laboratory Procedures for Technicians in Biopharmaceutical Analysis." *Amer. Lab.* 8, no. 8 (1976): 47–53.

Spriesterbach, D. C.; Hoppin, M. E.; and McCrone, J. "University Research and the New Federalism." *Science* 186 (1974): 324–327.

Straus, R. "Departments and Disciplines: Status and Change." *Science* 182 (1973): 895–898.

Supervisory Management Course, Part I: Supplemental Reading New York: American Management Association, 1968.

Tyler, V. E. "Admission and Placement of Foreign Graduate Students." *Amer. J. Pharm. Educ.* 41 (1977): 385–388.

Wertheimer, A. "Full Disclosure to Prospective Graduate Students." *Amer. J. Pharm. Educ.* 41 (1977): 391–393.

White, V. P. *Grants: How to Find Out about Them and What to Do Next.* New York: Plenum Press, 1975.

Wiesner, J. B. "Universities and the Federal Government: A Troubled Relationship." *Chem. Eng. News* 56, no. 50 (1978): 31–36.